CARIBBEAN

CARIBBEAN

PHOTOGRAPHY BY BOB KRIST • TEXT BY MARGARET ZELLERS

GRAPHIC ARTS CENTER PUBLISHING COMPANY, PORTLAND, OREGON

International Standard Book Number 1-55868-062-4
Library of Congress Number 91-71226
© MCMXCI by Graphic Arts Center Publishing Company
P.O. Box 10306 • Portland, OR 97210
President • Charles M. Hopkins
Editor-in-Chief • Douglas A. Pfeiffer
Managing Editor • Jean Andrews
Designer • Robert Reynolds
Cartographer • Manoa Mapworks, Inc.
Typographer • Harrison Typesetting, Inc.
Color Separations • Wy'east Color, Inc.
Printer • Rono Graphic Communications Co.
Bindery • Lincoln & Allen
Printed and bound in the United States of America

To my parents, Kris and Joyce, for giving me lots
   of guidance, but enough freedom to make my
   own decisions.
To my sons, Matt, Brian, and Jon, who accept their
   father's frequent absences with an understanding
   far beyond their years.
And most of all, to my wife, Peggy, whose love,
   grace, and good humour hold it all together.

BOB

To the many special people who have shared the
   Caribbean with me, especially my parents, my
   sister and brother-in-law, and my nephews, John
   and Geoffrey, who have helped me see familiar
   places in new and pleasing ways and have made
   warm memories out of otherwise routine events.

MARGARET

The Caribbean islands
are legendary, whether they are the top of a mountain
range that pierces the sea or a living coral community
whose earliest organisms provide the anchor for those
now being formed. The people and the places live—
not only unto themselves but also in our memories. ◄ ◄

THE CARIBBEAN

CUBA

**Santiago
de Cuba**

Great Inagua

Guantanamo

Windward Passage

JAMAICA

Kingston

Jamaica Channel

Cap-Haïtien

HAITI

CORDILLERA

CENTRAL

HISPANIOLA

DOMINICAN
REPUBLIC

Santiago

Santo Domingo

Port-au-Prince

MASSIF DU SUD

Jacmel

*Atlantic
Ocean*

LEEWARD ISLANDS

Mona Passage

Anegada Passage

ANGUILLA

Marigot • Anguilla
• St Martin (Fr/Neth)
St Barthélemy (Fr)

Saba (Neth)
St Eustatius (Neth)

ST
CHRISTOPHER
-NEVIS

St Christopher
(St Kitts)

Basseterre

Nevis

MONTSERRAT
(UK)
Montserrat

ANTIGUA
&
BARBUDA
(UK)

Barbuda

St John's Antigua

GUADELOUPE (Fr)

Grande Terre
Pointe-à-Pitre
Basse Terre

Marie Galante

Isles des Saintes

Guadeloupe Passage

DOMINICA (UK)
Dominica
TROIS PITONS
NP
Roseau

Dominica Passage

MARTINIQUE (Fr)

Martinique
Fort de France

St Lucia Channel

ST LUCIA (UK)
PIGEON IS NP St Lucia
Castries

St Vincent Passage

ST VINCENT St Vincent
&
THE
GRENADINES • **Kingstown**

Bequia

Canouan

THE GRENADINES
Carriacou

GRENADA

St George's • Grenada

BARBADOS

Bridgetown

WINDWARD ISLANDS

LESSER ANTILLES

VIRGIN ISLANDS
(USA/UK)

Anegada
Virgin
Tortola Gorda
St John
St Thomas ■ VIRGIN IS
**Charlotte NP
Amalie**
Vieques

St Croix

PUERTO RICO
(USA)

San Juan
Mayaguez • PUERTO RICO • **Ponce**
Mona

*Caribbean
Sea*

G R E A T E R

A N T I L L E S

*Islas Los
Testigos*

Margarita
• **Porlamar**

Islas Los
Hermanos

La Tortuga

Islas Los Roques

Bonaire

Curaçao
• Willemstad

Aruba

Islas de Aves

TRINIDAD
&
TOBAGO

Tobago

**Port of
Spain** ■ Trinidad
Trinidad

• **CARACAS**

VENEZUELA

Barquisimeto •

CORDILLERA DE BUENA VISTA

Gulf of Venezuela

Maracaibo •

SIERRA DE PERIJA

COLOMBIA

Barranquilla •

■ *National Park (NP)*

100 miles

0   50   100

0   50   100   150 kilometers

ATLANTIC
OCEAN

NORTH
AMERICA

Gulf of Mexico

WEST

Panama
Canal

*PACIFIC
OCEAN*

SOUTH
AMERICA

N
W—E
S

White sand, as soft as talcum powder, stretches as far as the eye can see. The only footprints along the beach are mine, on this first walk of the morning, and the only other marks on my path are from sea creatures that felt secure enough to forage in the pre-dawn stillness—or were tossed there by a roiling wave.

The sea that laps the shoreline, and sometimes my toes, is just about body temperature—slightly above or slightly below, depending on when and where I happen to swim, how deep I dive, how long it has been toasted by the Caribbean sunshine, and the time of the year. (The sea temperature varies about ten degrees from summer to winter.)

When I pause, to rest on the curve of a nearby palm tree's trunk, to listen to the rustle of its fronds in the gentle trade winds, I dig my toes into soft sand and stare out to sea. All's right with the world. If the scene is dotted with a sailboat or two, so much the better, but the view is sensational, even in waiting.

Life in the Caribbean seems serene. Perhaps that is its charm. Certainly that is part of it. But the region is curious with its contrasts. We dream of a place that is carefree, bathed in constant sunshine (except when it is blanketed by starlit nights), cooled by ever-present breezes, and decorated with sensational flowers set against verdant foliage. We see smiling people waiting to welcome us. We anticipate comfort and coddling.

But the Caribbean is also a region of violence, as the Arawaks discovered when they were invaded by the Caribs, and both the Arawaks and the Caribs found when they were set upon by the Spaniards, and the Spaniards learned from the British or the French (and vice versa), and so on through the islands' history. It is even true these days, although invasions have been limited to tourists since the Grenada action in 1983.

The Caribbean is a region where hurricanes have splintered buildings, broken trees like matchsticks, and given once-lush islands a brutal crew-cut in a few hours; where earthquakes have dumped thriving communities into the sea, like Jamaica's Port Royal in 1692; and where volcanoes have erupted, burying an entire town, as happened in Martinique in 1902.

Perhaps it is the contrasts that have given the islands their magic—the perfection of nature and the not-so-perfect lines of modern construction; the semblance of luxury and the West Indians' resentment of servitude; the complexions of people, from darkest ebony to sun-pinked white.

"Islomanes" is what Lawrence Durrell has called those of us addicted to islands, but no one has clearly defined the island appeal. What draws us to these specks in the sea? Is it the search for "paradise?" The lure of adventure? The temptation of new horizons? Is it the pursuit of a dream? Do we hope for a "perfect" place with a simpler, saner life? Were we all enchanted as children by Robinson Crusoe? Did we perceive Swiss Family Robinson to have the ideal lifestyle?

We search, like Diogenes looking for an honest man, for paradise; many ignore problems to find it in the Caribbean.

The finite boundaries of islands fool us into believing that islands are easy to understand. They are not. Especially in the Caribbean. The only certainty is that no two islands are exactly alike, even when they share a common government. History and natural attributes conspire to make each one different.

Just like people, each island has its own personality. Thus, once-British Jamaica is not like Puerto Rico with its Spanish heritage, even though nature has endowed them with similar characteristics and they are almost the same size.

And the Latino Dominican Republic is very different from the French-affected Haiti, although both share the island of Hispaniola. Dutch Sint Maarten is also different from French St. Martin, in spite of the fact that tourism has stomped with a heavy foot on the small island they share. And Nevis is different from St. Kitts, although the two islands are a single independent Caribbean country with a British heritage.

The Caribbean sea, an oval area about sixteen hundred miles east to west and seven hundred miles north to south, serves as a buffer between the south coast of the United States and the north coast of South America. Most of the islands are like pickets of a curving fence, separating the Atlantic Ocean from a sea cupped by the east coast of Central America.

Though there are hundreds of islands, only a few—Jamaica, the Cayman Islands, Mexico's Cozumel and Isla Mujeres, Colombia's San Andres, Venezuela's Margarita, and the Dutch-affiliated Aruba, Bonaire, and Curaçao among them—are entirely surrounded by the Caribbean Sea.

Most have either southern or western shores (sometimes both) washed by the Caribbean, and some—the islands of the Bahamas, Turks and Caicos, and Barbados—are surrounded by the Atlantic Ocean, although they share the history and the sun-struck lifestyle of their neighbors.

Some of the islands are independent countries. Haiti was the first. It became independent in 1804, followed by the Dominican Republic in 1844, and Cuba in 1898. These days, most of the islands are independent, having become so since 1962. A few islands are still dependent territories, albeit in a modern way that yanks them from the former "colony" status and gives each a strong measure of self-government.

Thus, Anguilla, the British Virgin Islands, the Cayman Islands, Montserrat, and Turks and Caicos islands are still British affiliated; the United States watches over the Commonwealth of Puerto Rico and the multi-island territory of the United States Virgin Islands (St. Croix, St. John, and St. Thomas); and the Netherlands government has a symbiotic relationship with Sint Maarten, Saba, Sint Eustatius, Aruba, Bonaire, and Curaçao.

Geologists suspect that a few of the northern islands—notably Cuba and Hispaniola—may have been part of the land-mass of eastern Mexico; and a few of the southern islands—Trinidad, for sure—broke from the coast of South America. But these mountainous islands are only part of the picture.

The "seven hundred islands" of the Bahamas, east and south of the tip of Florida, are basically flat with an occasional hill, and groves of feathery island pines in the few places where tourism, lumbering, and development have not mowed them away. The Turks and Caicos islands, separated by the twenty-two-mile-wide Columbus Passage, which plunges to a depth of seven thousand feet and was known as the Turks Islands Passage until recent renaming, are also flat and sand-fringed, with dramatic scenery under the sea where it is enjoyed by divers.

Cuba, less than ninety miles south of Florida's tip and stretching toward Mexico's Yucatan Peninsula, is the largest of the Caribbean islands. And Cuba plus Jamaica, Hispaniola, and Puerto Rico make up the Greater Antilles, a traditional term for the large islands that define, east to west, the northern rim of the Caribbean Sea. Each has a mountainous spine, where verdant

◄ *A proud bearing and a straight back help Haitians to use their heads.*

forests hide waterfalls, lakes, and endemic birds, and much of the interior's tropical growth is seldom, if ever, explored. The beaches that fringe some of the shoreline come in shades from butterscotch-brown to cornstarch-white. And hotels and resorts mark some, but by no means all, of the strands.

Puerto Rico's varied landscape—with foliage-covered mountains that drop to southern plains—is reflected, in smaller, less dramatic versions, on its satellite islands of Vieques and Culebra, and even the U.S. Virgin Islands (St. Croix, St. John, and St. Thomas). All lie farther east, as the start of the Lesser Antilles, a catch-all name for the rest of the Caribbean islands.

A cluster of islands—including the British and U.S. Virgins—are separated by the lively seas of Anegada Passage from flat-and-sandy Anguilla and resort-studded Sint Maarten/St. Martin, to the east, before the island chain begins its long reach south.

Saba and Sint Eustatius, Dutch-affiliated southern neighbors of Sint Maarten, are mostly cones of dormant volcanoes with verdant flanks that invite exploring. Although scuba divers are lured by shipwrecks and the sealife offshore, the beaches are not the best. (In the case of Saba, there are none worth the name.)

Beaches are better on Antigua, which is vaguely mountainous and rimmed with soft, white sand at almost every cove, and on Barbuda, its flat-as-a-pancake sister island that lies several miles northeast. There are also lovely beaches along the south coast of St. Kitts, where a recently opened, U.S.-financed scenic road carves the first paved land route down the length of the mountainous peninsula.

The northern sector of St. Kitts, as well as its sister island of Nevis, is marked by volcanic peaks, where slopes have nurtured once-British plantations that have become charming inns. Nearby British Montserrat is also a volcanic island, where soft, grey-to-black sand fringes a few of the most accessible shores, but beige sand borders a boat-reached cove.

The French department of Guadeloupe lies within view to the southeast. The "island" is actually two islands linked by a bridge, with the mountainous terrain of a lush volcanic island on western Basse-Terre and the flatter, sand-fringed landscape expected at beach resorts on eastern Grande-Terre. Its satellite of St. Barthelemy is far to the north, closer to Sint Maarten than to Guadeloupe. The eight tiny islands of the Iles des Saintes are off Guadeloupe's south coast; Marie-Galante lies east of Basse-Terre and south of Grande-Terre; and Le Desirade is slightly east of the northern part of Grande-Terre.

Dramatically different Dominica is the nearest neighbor heading south. Home to the purest surviving Carib community (there is another group on St. Vincent, and others live on Belize and Honduras), Dominica also has more breathtaking scenery and more endemic parrots (two species) than any other island. Dominicans (pronounced "Dough-min-EE-cans," not to be confused with like-spelled, Spanish-speaking "Do-MIN-nee-cans" from the Dominican Republic) share a creole language and commerce with their French neighbors, although the independent country follows a British style of government adapted from its former colonial power.

Mountainous Martinique, which shares creole customs and the colorful Madras traditional dress with its French relative, Guadeloupe, claims a newsmaking volcano, Mont Pelee. Its eruption destroyed the town of St. Pierre and sent shockwaves through the rest of the region. Its southern beaches and active marinas belie the terror of that time.

St. Lucia, whose dramatic twin peaks—the Pitons—are in sight of the south coast of Martinique, is next in the island chain. While its mountainous spine is wilderness and a few of its west coast beaches are flecked with resort hotels, St. Lucia's east coast and its lifestyle remain uniquely its own. French neighbors and a seesawing French and British colonial rule have knit the fabric of daily life.

Similar in terrain but with a volcanic peak in its northern sector, St. Vincent continues to move outside the tourism mainstream, developing the better beaches and surrounding seas of its Grenadine islands to the south for sailors, scuba divers, and other adventurers.

Grenada, at the far end of the string of tiny Grenadine islands and claiming two (Carriacou and Petit Martinique) as its own, is also volcanic. Its mid-island crater lake is a nature preserve, and its northern sector is virtually untouched. Tourism claims the south coast, where soft, white-sand beaches slope gently into the sea.

Barbados, in the southeast, is the first and only scout to face the Atlantic seas on their unchecked advance from African shores. Tourism has been a long-standing fact of life, not only for eighteenth-century British, eager to visit when winter winds whipped the British Isles, but also for George Washington, who visited his brother, Lawrence, here. Cane fields cover most of this coral island, but resorts are etched onto the west and south coasts, leaving the rugged, wind-buffeted east coast and mid-island sugar plantations as relief from development.

Trinidad and Tobago, one country with two distinct personalities, is a microcosm of Caribbean landscapes. While Trinidad's cosmopolitan capital of Port of Spain is home for a multi-racial population, most of the rest of the island is little known to outsiders. A nature center hides in the northern mountain range, flocks of scarlet ibis nest near the capital, and asphalt from mid-island pits was used to caulk the ships of Sir Francis Drake and pave the streets of towns in the United States.

Tobago, meanwhile, maintains a more traditional island style, with beige beaches, resort hotels, and a hinterland best known to birds and other natural residents. Its offshore reefs lure adventuresome divers.

A trio of Dutch-linked islands (Aruba, Bonaire, and Curaçao) sits off the Venezuelan coast to the west. Flat coral outcroppings with desertlike terrain, these islands are marked by unusual hills, caves known to the earliest settlers, and—in the case of Bonaire—a resident crop of flamingos that make the island their winter home.

And so it goes, from north to south, through the litany of the best-known vacation islands. But there are more. Margarita, to the north of mother-country Venezuela, is tied to a South American lifestyle, as are sleepy San Andres and its sister, Providencia (confused by some with Providenciales, far north in the Turks and Caicos islands). San Andres and Providencia are both Colombian.

Off the coast of Honduras, the Islas de la Bahia are known to sailors and scuba divers, most of whom focus on Roatan for expected comforts. The independent country of British-affiliated Belize is now being rediscovered by intrepid scuba divers and environmentalists. Its history, however, is firmly forged to the eastern islands.

Though all have been found—and named—many islands sleep under the Caribbean sun, far from familiar tourist routes. Modern comforts may not be in place, but nature's attributes

The twenty-ninth U.S. National Park, on Virgin Islands' St. John, has coves with sand as fine and white as powder. ▶

are refreshingly secure. The magic of untrammeled islands can still be enjoyed. The days for rediscoveries are dawning.

For me, it is the people that make the place. Even though I often return to the islands, it is the people who introduced me to these places that I remember when I am there—and that bring joy to my memories when I am away. Several years ago, in a closet-sized atelier in the slightly scruffy warren of shops that grew on eighteenth-century pirate warehouse walls in downtown St. Thomas, there was an elderly man who nurtured metal into fine jewelry.

By the time I met him, he was nearly blind, but Mr. Callwood appeared in his shop most mornings, to create fine jewelry in the warm sun splashing through his open window. For years, I have worn the gold bracelet he made in his version of the ancient slave bracelets; and for years I have remembered his tales of childhood life on that now-frantic U.S. Virgin Island, where shoppers surge most days, unchecked except by the size of their bank account, in search of treasures.

The islands were still Danish when Mr. Callwood was a boy. They became American in 1917, when the U.S. government bought them for $25 million, as a buffer in time of war. Coming to town was a big occasion for people who lived on the far side of the island, less than three miles away. It meant walking or riding a donkey for most people, following a serpentine, unpaved route up and over the mountain spine. Cars were scarce; commerce, negligible. It would be several years before cruise ships and tourism would become a daily fact of life.

Even by the late 1950s, there were none of the traffic jams that now clog the waterfront road—and few of the hotels that now embroider most sandy coves. People made time for polite conversation, which always began with proper greetings: a long and thoughtful "Good morning," "Good afternoon," or "Good evening," depending on the time of day. And the greeting always earned a considered and pleasant response, most often accompanied by a smile.

That is still the case on some islands, where commerce has not yet caught the plague of more cosmopolitan centers. On Dominica, for example, I recently spent the better part of a day with Henry, who returned last year from London, where he had been studying law. He chose to come home with his family, to make his living on Dominica. He has also chosen to follow Rastafarian beliefs, giving his two young sons African names and wrapping his long-and-gnarled dreadlocks in a gauzelike turban that suggests Sikh Indian style. He continues to pursue his study of law, intending to draft environmental legislation—before the Caribbean landscape is irrevocably changed.

In tandem, he guides visitors into the verdant mountains of his homeland, sharing knowledge of his country's rich heritage—and contributing to the family coffers. His wife works in her parents' business, which includes two family-designed hotels, a watersports and diving operation, and other tourism ventures, in addition to the construction business that had been her father's original trade.

It was midday when Henry and I left the spent markets of the tiny capital of Roseau, and not long after that, we paused to pick up the first flock of teenagers on their way from school. On school days they walk for more than an hour each direction, hoping from time to time that a passing car will speed them on their way. Henry provided the "schoolbus" this day.

As our jeep bumped along the west coast road from Roseau toward Portsmouth, the sun sprinkled diamonds on the sea, and waves foaming on the road-rimmed shore sometimes sent salt spray through the open windows. Our car was propelled as much by a chorus of Dominica's national anthem as by Henry's foot on the accelerator. Laughter joined tidbits of conversation and interrupted the songs. From Justline, Claudette, Gail, and their friends, I learned about their school, their studies, and their dreams—and they left me with names and addresses, in hope of finding pen friends in my native land.

Other days on other islands, I pick up school children in my rental car, to learn from them as I drive them to or from school. Always they are tidy in their uniforms, dictated by traditional British custom, though adapted to the vagaries of Caribbean life. Sometimes blue and yellow, other times beige and brown or another combination, the uniforms come in all sizes and shapes. In at least one case, the girls' red skirts and boys' red trousers, topped with white shirts, were chosen for the colors of the Canadian flag, in gratitude because Canada had financed their school, just north of Castries, St. Lucia's capital.

"Aaa-mi-zon-ah ver-si-coe-lour" may not seem like appropriate words to start a lilting melody, but when a couple of dozen preteens begin their song, weaving like sugar cane in a tropical breeze as they sing their way through three verses, the tune hangs forever in memory. "Amazona Versicolor" is the national bird of St. Lucia, better known to local folk as "Jacquot," a large and colorful parrot. The song, sung to a calypso beat, is one of their favorites, learned as a subtle part of a national pride campaign that includes sermons in churches and other songs that have become popular disco dancing tunes.

As recently as 1977, the St. Lucian Parrot flirted with extinction. Once common, the parrot population was down to about a hundred. The birds' natural forest habitat had been gradually destroyed, cleared for fields of sugar cane and other crops, for living areas for an expanding population, as well as to use for fuel and lumber. By 1987, after a decade of intense conservation efforts by the St. Lucian Forestry Department, the parrot population had increased to almost two hundred fifty birds. As a result of conservation efforts since that time, the parrot population continues to increase, as the habitat has been saved. Another benefit has been local awareness about how fragile island landscapes can be preserved and enhanced.

Since April 1991, a colorful bus wheezes and lurches its way into the countryside, squawking like a parrot when prodded to do so by the driver. Painted on the outside is a mural of parrot life; the interior is a schoolroom, dedicated to explaining—with the help of a Forestry Department teacher, through dioramas, games, and creative other ploys—the importance of saving the forest.

The bus is a joint venture between the St. Lucia Forestry Department who will operate it, the British-based World Parrot Trust, and the Philadelphia-based RARE Center who conceived, funded, and fitted it. Its job is to take the conservation message to farmers and others in the countryside.

Endangered species and protection of the environment are the focus for RARE Center projects on several islands, always with the involvement of the local residents. Noting that rare bird species and the island's ecosystem are threatened by population growth, farming, tourism, lumbering, and other factors, islanders have been encouraged, often with RARE Center programs as the catalyst, to protect the Montserrat oriole,

◄ *The people of the Caribbean share their rich heritage through smiles, conversations, and customs.*

(*Icterus oberi*) and parrots such as the *Amazona guildingii* of St. Vincent; the *Amazona imperialis* and *Amazona aurasoaca* of Dominica; and the Cayman Islands parrot and the Bahamas parrot, both subspecies of the *Amazona leucocephala*, popularly known as the Cuban Parrot.

Monique came directly from Bahamas Community College to her conservation work with Bahamas Forestry Department. When she visits the schools and other congregating centers, she will be guided by the RARE Center program that includes puppet shows, songs, games, and other activities to make the parrot and his peril meaningful to the daily life of the islands. For the Bahamas, the bird has special importance: it was noted by Columbus when he arrived on San Salvador, claimed by most as the European traveler's first Caribbean landfall in 1492.

But the Bahamas are the nesting ground for many birds. In early morning on Crooked Island, if you look south toward Long Cay, you may see *Phoenicopterus ruber*, West Indian pink flamingos, as they fly from their marshland feeding areas to the sand banks. They are common around Inagua Island as well.

The saline waters in which flamingos find the algae food that keeps them pink are the same waters ideal for the salt industry that gave many islands their early prosperity. But, since flocks of wild flamingos linger only where people are not, the arrival of Morton Salt Company on Inagua in 1954, when they purchased a family business, was greeted with apprehension.

Local folks feared the worst, even though they were pleased that the revitalized salt harvesting had caught the eye of international entrepreneurs. Morton Salt proved to be a good neighbor, however, both in deed and in fact. They have maintained some of the salt marshes favored by the birds and have donated significant sums to the Bahamas National Trust for the National Park that is a habitat for many water birds.

Likewise on Bonaire, commercial ventures have proved compatible with wildlife preserves. On the island's southern tip, the Antilles International Salt Company has set aside a flamingo sanctuary, although some birds seem to prefer the company's well-tended salt pans as their restaurant-of-choice.

On other islands, there are other birds—and other environmental concerns. Trinidad has its flocks of scarlet ibis that nest at the Caroni Bird Sanctuary, not far from the country's capital of Port of Spain. And toucans, squirrel cuckoos, and other birds make their home in its Asa Wright Nature Centre, at Spring Hill Estate. Located in the northern mountain range, it is an area that continues to thrive away from the mainstream of development.

Tobago, marked for expanded tourism development by its government authorities, is home to hundreds of birds in its little-known interior, but the once-thriving bird of paradise, imported to a small island off the southern shore, vanished long ago. Only its name remains, as the tag for an island dot.

Children cluster around the ice-cone cart in the shade near the gates of Jamaica's Hope Botanical Gardens. Adults either yield or lead them away with a promise of "later"—after a stroll through portions of the two-hundred-acre park given to the country by the Hope family, soon after the abolition of slavery, in the mid-1800s. Sunday is the day Kingstonians come to picnic, walk, read, or ride the merry-go-round in the park, but the area is open daily. The Blue Mountains, namesake for the pungent coffee

that grows on the upper slopes, rise as an impressive backdrop. They peak at seven thousand feet.

Although Jamaica's capital of Kingston is a busy, sometimes raucous, city and Old Hope Road can be a traffic-clogged artery that makes it easy to miss the garden's gates, an hour's visit is a step into the real life of Jamaica, away from the tourist troughs.

"I used to wear a blue serge suit when we came here after church on Sundays," my friend Bill Whiting confessed, as a small child pranced by in her sunsuit. "And we used to play hide-and-seek over there," he said, pointing to a labyrinth of hedges that is a standard element in most traditional English gardens. The poui tree, jubilant in its cascade of lemon-yellow blossoms, stood alone on a grassy lawn, which was "better manicured when we came here as children," Bill said.

"The stream ran full in those days," he noted, as we stepped over a rut that may gurgle after a heavy rainfall. The orchid house is now enclosed with an ugly fence and the "display" during our visit was pathetic, but folks who coursed along the paths or lounged under the shade trees didn't seem to care. They were having fun—easily.

Since the late 1950s, while Caribbean countries have been grappling with the vagaries of independence, botanic gardens and other remnants from colonial life have fallen into disrepair. Only recently have national trust associations, forestry departments, and their ilk had the time (and training) to restore and maintain the legacy.

And just in time. Although much has been lost and extensive maintenance is an expensive proposition that still craves funding, Caribbean countries now realize the value of the God-given natural assets that make them what they appear to be: spectacular settings in a sparkling sea.

Although they are assumed to be indigenous, most blossoms that add drama and delight are not. They are merely tourists who took up permanent residence. Some seeds and plants came in the canoes and rafts of the earliest island settlers, from the mainland of North America as well as from South and Central America. But the migration began in earnest when Columbus reached these shores.

In the style of other early explorers, Columbus's ships carried plants for food en route. Later ships would bring the favorite produce from older colonies to the new ones. Thus, ginger made its way from Indonesia; and congea, known as "shower of orchids" on some islands, from Burma. Bougainvillea, named for French navigator Louis de Bougainville, was brought from Brazil; and the bright red poinsettia that blooms profusely at the Christmas season comes from Mexico. The dramatic bird of paradise, with its orange cockscomb and brilliant "beak," is native of South Africa. Heliconia, with its claw-like brackets, was brought from South America and now grows wild on Trinidad, Tobago, and many other islands.

The African tulip tree that Palisot Beauvois noted on the Gold Coast of Africa in 1787 is known by several names throughout the islands. Many believe that it has supernatural powers—as well it might—with its towering height, brilliant red blossom clusters, and boat-shaped seed pods. The cottonwood tree also plays a role in island lore as a home for *jumbies*, those spirits that hide in its tangled growth and cavort under its shelter when it rains.

Of all island trees, the dark green, waxy-leaved breadfruit, with its fruit of bowling-ball size, leads with legends. Captain Bligh of Bounty fame brought the seeds to the Caribbean.

"Jacquot" is what St. Lucians call their endemic parrot, now protected by Forestry Department and RARE Center efforts. ►

Whether or not he planted the tree that still stands in the Botanic Garden in Kingstown, St. Vincent, is a matter of speculation, but that he brought the fruit that has become the staple for West Indian diets from Africa is documented fact.

Just as their colonizing was widespread throughout the Caribbean, where most islands and some countries along the Caribbean coast of Central America claim British heritage, so the British also brought their love of botany. They established most of the botanic gardens on Jamaica and on Trinidad, Barbados, St. Vincent, St. Lucia, and Grenada, where they stand today as testimony to British zeal. St. Vincent's King's Hill Forest Reserve, for example, was defined and chartered in 1791, and Dominica's Botanic Gardens near Roseau were established in 1890, although hurricane damage and other exigencies have modified the importance of both.

The lush rain forests—with their cool, moist climate; their broad-leafed planting in shades of green too numerous to count; and their unique, often endangered, species of birds and other fauna—are the special secret of the Caribbean. While Puerto Rico's El Yunque makes a name for itself as host to the only tropical forest under U.S. Forestry Department jurisdiction, there are many verdant and little-known mountainous areas on that island.

Dominica's fertile forest, portions of which are habitat for the Imperial Parrot that is its national bird, is the largest and most complex rain forest on the Caribbean islands, but there are also verdant areas on Cuba, the Dominican Republic, Guadeloupe, Martinique, St. Lucia, and St. Vincent. Belize is unique with its seldom-explored hinterland, and even developed St. Croix has a rain forest, flourishing out of the mainstream, in a north-western pocket of land.

But not all the islands are lush and green, with vast, natural tropical forests. St. Croix, with a rain forest in one part, slopes to a dry, desertlike peninsula at its easternmost point. Some islands are arid, such as the Dutch-affiliated ABCs—Aruba, Bonaire, and Curaçao—in the southern Caribbean, where the coral limestone islands appear like splinters off the Venezuelan coast. The Watapana tree, permanently bent at a 90-degree angle by the prevailing winds, is better known on Aruba as the DiviDivi tree, the island's national symbol.

On arid islands—or parched portions of islands with varied landscape—cacti bloom, sometimes in groves as in Curaçao's Cristoffel National Park, and elsewhere in isolation, as on most dry islands where the unusual blossoms look as though they have been stuck onto the cactus by some outside force. (The egg shells you may see "growing" on the spikes of cactus plants are a popular West Indian houseplant decoration.)

Ilodalik's fingers curled like brackets on the frame of the open car window. Rain coursed over his thatch of shiny black hair, making waterfalls from his nose and eyebrows. His eyes gleamed like orbs of coal; his smile was wide and white-toothed, when my questions (or the way I looked) prompted him to make one. Ilodalik is a Carib, he's seven, his eyes sparkle, and he loves the rain. I loved the shelter inside the car, and the sound of his voice, when I asked him where he lived ("up the hill"), why he wasn't in school ("don't go"), and where his friends had gone when they scattered as I slowed my car on the rutted road ("to get fish"). Our brief encounter—not more than ten minutes, in the Carib community of Dominica—is one of my favorite memories.

Ilodalik is now a grown man. Life in his community has changed, but not beyond recognition. A few older folks still split and weave narrow bands of Wacine-palmiste and vines into fine, firm baskets and make bird cages from Woseau reed once used for arrow shafts. And the skin of bamboo is still woven into fishpots and landing scoops by some fishermen, although most have turned to plastic line and chicken wire for the tools of their trade.

The Caribs and their customs are very much a part of the domestic island life, and their name lives on in the name of the region, whether you choose to pronounce it "Carib-BE-an" or "Ca-RIB-be-an." (Both are correct.)

The islands of the West Indies, so named by Christopher Columbus in his search for the *East* Indies, were an earlier landfall for Arawaks, Tainos, Ciboneys, and other tribes. Their settlements in the Bahamas, north of the Caribbean Sea, and on the Caribbean's Puerto Rico, Cuba, Antigua, and other islands are testimony, through their artifacts, to a pattern of living that included ballparks, round thatched-roof dwellings, and a communal life that led the women to yield to the Caribs, although some scholars believe they never learned their conquerors' language.

The first tribes made their way from Venezuela's Orinoco River, north and then west from island to island. Others may have come from the west from settlements in Central America, and from the north. Peaceful tribes were conquered, first by the Caribs, who destroyed the gentler culture with their more aggressive ways, and then by the Spaniards who used Arawaks brought from Aruba for arduous field work in their settlements on the Dominican Republic.

As thirteen-year-old Andre told me who built what and why, he slouched at the feet of Christopher Columbus. Columbus stands firmly, as he has since the French cast him in bronze in 1837, on Plaza Colon, outside the buttery-beige Cathedral de Santa Maria la Menor, in the old city of Santo Domingo, the capital of the Dominican Republic.

And Cristobal Colon, as he is known in Spain, began to weave a colorful tapestry of European-Caribbean culture when he arrived on the north coast of Hispaniola (La Española) in 1492, after first landing in the Bahamas. On his second voyage, in 1493, Columbus returned with fifteen hundred men in seventeen ships, sighting Dominica on November 3 and noting—and naming—Guadeloupe, St. Martin, Antigua, Montserrat, Santa Cruz (now known as St. Croix), and Puerto Rico (rich port), which he called San Juan. After establishing a settlement at Isabela on La Española, the voyage continued on to Jamaica, where his ships wrecked on the north coast, east of Runaway Bay.

On his third voyage, with six ships in 1498, Columbus found Trinidad and the coast of South America, where he explored the mouth of the Orinoco. The fourth voyage, in 1502, resulted in the sighting of St. Lucia, before he went on to the riches of Central America.

Andre is one of the street children who swarm around the sights of ancient Santo Domingo, eager to take you on a walking tour—for a few pesos. His paces locked with mine as I stepped from the taxi; his bright black eyes and spontaneous smile were his ticket to my heart. Though his dates might be flawed, his enthusiasm made his companionship comfortable.

It struck me that his jaunty step and apparent confidence had its echo in the past, when Diego Colon, Christopher's son,

◄ *St. Lucia's Pitons are impressive landmarks, made even more dramatic with a rainbow garland and flowering trees.*

had been viceroy of Santo Domingo—in the 1500s. Then, workmen Andre's age had piled block upon limestone block to make the buildings we marvel at today, before, in many cases, they sailed on to Mexico and elsewhere in Central America, to build cathedrals and other structures there.

Santo Domingo is unique, as a thriving twentieth-century city that has grown, like barnacles, on the fringes of a sixteenth-century core. To stroll along Calle de las Damas in the golden light of afternoon, as sixteenth-century ladies did, is to walk through history. Following a street plan of the early 1500s, many structures have been rebuilt in the style of that time, using limestone from original quarries. Others have been restored, and all are revitalized to bring the past into the present.

Santo Domingo has its counterpart in Puerto Rico's San Juan, spawned from the Dominican Republic settlement. Authentic to its time because the fort-protected peninsula made expansion on the three water-locked sides impossible, the historic buildings of Old San Juan nurture culture. The Dominican Convent is a historic building that hosts exhibitions by Puerto Rican artists; the gemlike museum of famed cellist Pablo Casals nestles in a contiguous building; and dozens of seventeenth-century balconied buildings hold museums, boutiques, cafes, and art galleries in their carefully restored locations on the narrow streets of the old city.

La Fortaleza, built in 1540, continues to be the headquarters for the island administrator—the governor of the United States Commonwealth who is elected by the Puerto Rican population. Its neighbor, Casa Blanca, a home built for Ponce de Leon, who went from here to Florida, is a museum by day and the site for occasional outdoor concerts. And the town's many plazas host festivals and fetes, sometimes spontaneous and often linked to saints' days on this largely Catholic island.

Although the Spanish came first, leaving behind a legacy of language, customs, art, and architecture, they are by no means the only Europeans to make a permanent mark on the region. Dozens of forts stand as testimony to the importance that the Spanish, English, French, and Dutch put on the area. This is where they fought significant sea and land battles during the seventeenth and eighteenth centuries while they strove to claim the best parcels among the new world discoveries.

Brimstone Hill is perched on a limestone bluff on the west coast of St. Kitts, with a view that includes St. Barthelemy, Sint Maarten, and Nevis. It has its echo at the Citadelle on the north coast of Haiti, where hundreds of Haitians lost their lives between 1805 and 1820 while building an impregnable bastion against the French, on orders from Henri Christophe, Kittitian by birth and the first king of Haiti.

Fort St. Louis, worked into the waterfront of today's Fort-de-France, protected the harbor for the French on Martinique. Fort Charles, now an integral part of a modern hotel, stood watch on the southern rim of Bridgetown, Barbados. Fort Young, built onto the bluff overlooking Roseau, is masked by a hotel on Dominica, while that country's Fort Shirley, in a 260-acre national park on the Cabrits headland north of Portsmouth, houses a maritime museum. Shirley Heights on Antigua, built for a British garrison, commands a bird's-eye view of English Harbour, where the British Navy's Caribbean fleet was based. Admiral Nelson gave his name to the dockyard, now restored and alive with yachts.

They skirmished on the high seas, but the British also settled several islands from Jamaica to Trinidad, including Antigua, Barbados, St. Kitts, St. Vincent, St. Lucia, and others. They planted sugar cane, creating plantations punctuated by the Great Houses that have become elegant private homes, lovely inns, romantic restaurants, or gentle museums where afternoon tea is served on the terrace in the shade of a cottonwood tree.

They brought Georgian architecture into the Caribbean, where local craftsmen adapted it to the warmer climate with balconies on buildings, a roofline suitable for deflecting the sun's strong rays, and louvered windows to open for tradewind air-conditioning (and close when winds are strong). Furniture styles from the home country were worked in Jamaican mahogany and other wood, adapted for tropical use with woven cane that lets welcomed breezes through the chairbacks.

The French, who set their sights on settlements in the West Indies, mingled more than their European colleagues with the Caribs and the Africans who were brought from far off shores to cultivate the cane and other crops. From France came the language, the creole customs, and a recipe for life that leads to style, spices, and skilled preparation of island staples that dress the tables at mealtimes and delight the palate.

Dutch ways—neatness, a keen business sense, a style of fair play—are very much a part of the Netherlands Antilles, not only with the sun-washed, gabled buildings that border streets in Curaçao's Willemstad, but also with the Indonesian food and warm-weather customs brought from the Dutch East Indies.

Scandinavians, too, set their sights on the West Indies. The Danes settled the U.S. Virgin Islands, which they owned until the early twentieth century, leaving forts and architecture, as well as street plans, in the towns of Christiansted and Frederiksted on St. Croix, and in Charlotte Amalie, the group's capital on St. Thomas. Swedes settled St. Barthelemy, giving the tiny, U-shaped capital its name—Gustavia—in honor of the Swedish king, and its people their fair complexions.

And so it is that Columbus's followers—from pirates to plantocracy, Spaniards, French, English, Dutch, Danes, and especially the Africans, Chinese, and Indians brought to work the plantations—carried fragments from their home countries to weave into the rich tapestry on these sun-struck shores.

The spice of the islands comes from many sources. It is not just the Keshi Yena, a fat, stuffed cheese shell that melts into its seasoned filling. Or the rijsttafel that early Dutch settlers brought from their East Indies to the similarly hot climate of the West Indies. Or the pepper sauce that looks innocuous, but can send tears cascading down your cheeks when it sears your throat with its fiery essence.

The spice of the Caribbean is all of these and much more. It is thick, mud-green callaloo soup, piping hot and pungent. And it is peppery stuffed crab backs, using the land crabs that skitter across the road and around their hole-in-the-ground homes, lured out on dark nights by a flame torch—or a flashlight, if you're rich enough to have one. It is mountain chicken, as the large frogs of tropical forests are called when they appear, cooked and savoury, at the mealtime table. And it's curried goat.

It is lambi, with bits of conch made tender by careful pounding, perhaps between shell-and-stone on the beach where the shellfish is brought ashore by fishermen who dive deep to yank them off the ocean floor. And it's blaff, a fish stew served on the French islands, where cooks cut the fresh catch, to simmer it

Dominica is etched with waterfalls, creating myriad pools such as the Emerald Pool in Morne Trois Pitons National Park. ▶

in pieces, with kitchen herbs and spices. Blaff is best when served with crusty, warm, fresh-baked bread—and wine.

Grenada calls itself the "Spice Island," for the nutmegs, mace, and other seasonings grown on its hills and exported to provide hard currency for its coffers. But spices have been important crops on many islands, dating from the time when seventeenth- and eighteenth-century travelers brought them home to give flavor to the best tables of Europe.

And they continue to be important ingredients in the best Caribbean restaurants, which might be an extension of someone's kitchen, sometimes at seaside, other times nestled in a verdant grove on a hillside. Memorable places are those where the cook serves at a few tables on her porch, at a shack just off the road. Or by the clear Caribbean, at an open-to-breezes bistro, where you can dress in your bathing suit and use the sea as your finger bowl. Or at a local gathering spot, perhaps a rum shop, where you can order a "Ti punch" with the fishermen.

"Ti punch," like many rum drinks, is hard to forget. Unique to the French islands, it is a potent mixture of strong rum, sweet sugar syrup, and a squeeze of fresh lime, properly served with a ceremony reminiscent of British high tea. It is sipped, while socializing—or simply daydreaming.

When sugar was the islands' main crop, rum was the extract from its fermented juices. And rum these days is an island staple, mixed, whipped, and cajoled—sometimes with fruit juices—into an assortment of drinks. Some of us think it's best when simply served—neat—so you can enjoy the unique shade of gold, and the flavor that comes with each distilling style.

The essence of Caribbean life comes from more than the kitchen or the bar, however. It comes with the lifestyle. While some islands seem ready to leap into the twentieth century, others are content with their longtime traditions. Local produce yields the best meals, but it can also be a fashion statement! It often appears as a "hat," on countryfolk who use their heads to carry home-grown provisions to and from the marketplace.

That is the case on Haiti, or St. Lucia, or St. Vincent, or any one of several other islands still removed from the well-traveled routes for tourism. Women of proud bearing cap themselves with their parcels, walking miles to market, as much for the social event as for the money they will get from the sale of their produce.

On French Guadeloupe, at the August *Fête des Cuisiniéres,* culinary specialties are carried—on heads and in outstretched arms—to be presented for the Cathedral blessing. The lady-chefs, whose often-ample shapes suggest that they enjoy their cooking, wear Creole costumes as they dance in the streets in celebration of a successful fete.

By way of contrast to a fete with complex recipes, consider the specialists such as Mr. Rodriguez, in southwestern Puerto Rico, who stands near his roadside table-board of pineapples, awaiting a passer-by. On the day I found him, he stepped toward me with the dignity of a maitre d'hotel, offering a sun-warmed pineapple that perfumed my car when I cut it—and sent sweet juice down my throat when I bit.

Though pineapples are a specialty on Puerto Rico, Antigua, and a few other islands, fresh fruits and vegetables are piled in colorful pyramids along the country roads, as well as at market-places, on many islands.

In Jamaica, for example, there are heaps of red-skinned ackee, split to reveal the yellow pulp that's cooked for the traditional Jamaican breakfast. And golden-orange mangoes are clustered, as are various kinds of bananas, plus star-apples, gnips, and other tropical fruit, when they are in season. (Mangoes are best enjoyed by the beach, where you can wash away the flood of juice that bursts forth when you bite.)

These are the riches of the islands, today's treasures, to savour on the spot—and carry away as memories.

For many in the Caribbean, music is the food of life. West Indians are born with melodies in their souls. Their movement is as natural as that of trees in the trade winds, set to motion at the first note of a lilting tune played on the radio or when two or three are gathered together and have a potential instrument at hand. "If Trinnies would put half as much effort into running their country as they put into their carnival, they'd have the greatest country in the world," a Trinidadian friend told me long ago. You have only to visit a 'Mas Camp, as the gathering spots for various carnival bands are known, to appreciate what he means.

When the Desperadoes play, their music fills the sky. It was after midnight when our van wound up Laventille Hill, in a part of Port of Spain not on the usual tourist track. Warm light came from shacks along the roadside; faces dotted windows; and people hung against the walls, clustering like moths to flame around the doorways of rum shops. As we lurched along the snake-route up the hill, assorted rocks and ruts tried to scrape the underpinnings from the van. That was our only peril.

In the clearing where they played, the band's leader sat on a throne of wooden boxes, a whale of a woman swathed in gossamer white, with her hair hidden in a bathing-cap style that made her appear high-fashion. Her baton, which she waved like a fairy-godmother's wand, coaxed haunting melodies from more than one hundred steel oil drums, cut, tempered, and tuned, to be played to symphony standards by as many as seventy men and women. (The instrument was invented in the 1940s, when American military folk stationed on Trinidad began a fad of slicing the ends off oil drums, to heat-and-tap the ends into tonal bumps, to be played like a xylophone.)

By November, dozens of panyards are already in full tone, practicing for Trinidad's pre-Lenten carnival, the granddaddy of all Caribbean carnivals—and an event mentioned in the same breath with Rio's pre-Lenten bash.

Although it is the Caribbean's biggest and best, it is by no means the only. Tradition places carnival as a final fling before the six weeks of austerity and penitence demanded by the Christian calendar, but practical considerations have moved Caribbean carnivals to other times. Jamaica has its in June, Antigua's is in August, St. Vincent's is in May, all held when tourism's demands are less and life allows for celebration.

During one spring on Jamaica, witches giggled with clowns, while Indians eyed parrots near the elevators in the lobby of one of Kingston's high-rise hotels. Within minutes, relationships were severed as children were sucked into the minivans that carried them to the start of the children's parade.

Although the concerts that are evening events draw hundreds of Jamaican adults and friends, this is the children's chance. It is their introduction to the ritual of fete that will be forever a part of their life, when folks of all ages, creeds, and skin colors from ebony to powder-white would weave and wiggle on the sun-baked streets of Kingston, bringing laughter to their route through an otherwise sleeping-on-Sunday city.

◄ *To protect their settlement from English and French invasions, Spaniards built Puerto Rico's Fort San Cristobal in 1772.*

"The fete is definitely part of our life. The fun, the festival, the carnival, is used to cover so many sorrows," the artistic director and principal choreographer of Jamaica's pace-setting National Dance Theatre Company observed.

Today's carnivals and fetes take their cue from slave celebrations, which mimicked the grand quadrilles and the other dances at the master's Great House. The slaves gave their fetes special style, however, with African tribal rhythms and pent-up exuberance. It was a time when music and pantomime were the most effective means for often-forbidden communication.

Whether it's the tourist-conscious efforts of the Goombay celebrations at Nassau in the Bahamas, or the creative and cultural events at Crop-Over Festival on Barbados, today's celebrations are colorful, enthusiastic, often tuneful, and sometimes downright noisy. But over-all, they're fun!

On a few islands, music takes on a life of its own, as is the case with steel bands on Trinidad. And on Jamaica, Bob Marley's reggae permeates the air, coming into full bloom during an August festival in Montego Bay. On Puerto Rico, classical music sets the tone at the annual Casals festival, which takes place in June and fills weeks with symphonies and other events honoring the life of famed cellist, Pablo Casals, who left Franco's Spain for Puerto Rico—and died there in 1973.

On Aruba and Barbados, jazz festivals are prominent on the social calendar. And the Dominican Republic has its Merengue Festival, when Latins move as only they can to the dance some claim was created when President Trujillo had to dance with a stiff leg. His followers copied him—most gracefully.

As for dancing style on many islands, the best choreography integrates events in the life of traditional village and plantation workers into smoothly orchestrated movement that tells a rich story. The Groupe Folklorique that performs for cruise passengers and at hotels does it best on Martinique. But it is the zouk, a musical mingling of Caribbean rhythms and Creole words, that livens discos and other dance depots on that island.

Just as the islands have different physical characteristics, one from the other, so also their musical tastes reflect each island's unique personality—in spite of a sometimes overwhelming layer of "Yellow Bird," reggae, and rap throughout the region.

Boat-building in Caribbean communities has always been more than a job. It has been a labor of love as well as a matter of survival. For centuries, boats provided the only link with the outside world. The birth of one was greeted with more enthusiasm, in some places, than a newborn child. The beachside christening was a fete beyond belief, when home-brewed rum and other potions joined souse, callaloo, fresh-caught fish and all the village folk for a festive day—or days.

The big and bulky "Friendship Rose" was built on Bequia and, when launched, was the only "dependable" transportation between that island and St. Vincent. Its coffee-colored sails fit like baggy britches, but the wind carried the sturdy hull through the seas with a steady motion unknown by modern motorcraft.

Crates of chickens, limes, Coca Cola, and other necessities took precedence over the few passengers bound for one of the outpost inns. The spanking breeze that whipped through the open channel added chop to the always lively seas—and an unanticipated saltwater shower for most passengers.

A lunge was the best way to board the "Friendship Rose." Gracefulness was quickly forgotten; survival took precedence. Wandering along the waterfront and asking was the only way to learn departure times. And as for luggage, without a spoken word, every passenger knew you didn't take much—unless you were a belonger or making a major house move. Arrival was an adventure in those days, but a new airport is certain to yank local folk into the twentieth century with a lurch.

Villagers on some islands—Dominica, the Grenadines, and others out of the mainstream—still burn-and-carve-out the straight trunk of the gommier tree to make sturdy canoes. And there are boat builders who still frame up their craft on shore, working tirelessly to coax soaked boards to the bow of the hull. If you have the chance, watch a skeleton become a boat, as plank after plank is bent by pressure, to be fixed to an appropriate strut, perhaps by a modern nail but always capped with a wooden plug. Although the technique is older than many old-timers remember, it may soon disappear in a fleet of fiberglass.

The Family Islands of the Bahamas can trace their sport of sailing back to 1898, when races were held out of Long Island. These days, that country's Bahamian schooners, sloops, and dinghies sail out of Georgetown, in the Exuma Islands, competing in the annual Family Island Regatta or one of many regattas for Bahamian boats. Many of the home-built boats sport oversized sails that look like sheets on the laundry line and a complement of crew that could sink a less-sturdy craft. But none has more fun than the sea-doused competitors, for whom a spontaneous dunking can be part of the lark.

A counterpart to that race is the annual Carriacou Regatta, held out of Grenada's satellite island on August 1, and other races such as those held from Anguilla's shores. One of the most popular annual sailing events is Antigua's Race Week, when boats converge from around the Caribbean, skippered by top international competitors as well as seasoned island folk.

The joy of the Caribbean is that anyone can sail. Proficient sailors charter in the British Virgins, fondly called the playpen for sailing folk, or in the Grenadines, where heavier seas surge between the several islands and prevailing winds are strong, or in any of the marinas that fleck deep coves on the islands.

Then there are the divers. Most mornings, Adam rows his home-carved boat toward the horizon, following a path painted by the first rays of sun. When he sets out from his beachside hut the goal looks far away, but when you're sharing the fragile space in his beloved boat, the tiny offshore island looms larger as he rows closer. Once there, Adam sets his rock-anchor and slithers over the side, to free-dive—deep—to the nests of conch whose emptied shells he later plants by the side of his house. Soon he surfaces with a glove of conch that he stows on the sole of his boat, before he dives deep again for another.

To visitors who walk the length of Anguilla's Road Bay, Adam offers the cleaned conch shells for sale. Or he may just give the shells away. His life is a simple one by U.S. mainland standards, but he works diligently to eke his living from the sea—with the conch meat he sells to fellow Anguillians and to a few restaurants down the beach where visitors create the market.

While most of us will don scuba or snorkel gear before we free-dive, when surrounding seas are clear as crystal and colors range from aquamarine to sapphire, the temptation to get on it, under it, or at least in it is almost irresistable. Islands are like that. Nothing less than total immersion satisfies—and then you can hold the experiences in your heart forever.

Costumes and carnival capers are an integral part of Caribbean life, whether on Trinidad or another island. ▶

Religion knits the fabric of life for many island people, not only for those who were wrenched from Africa but also for European and other settlers who looked to the church to ease the way through difficult times. ◄ West Indian buildings gain their personality from the carpenter's skill and from the creativity—and the color choice—of the painter. ▲ The salt that provides the livelihood for the people of Inagua also lures flocks of flamingos, who gain their pink color from the algae that flourish in the salt flats. ► ►

Lighthouses have guided ships through treacherous coral reefs since the 1700s; a few still provide work for people like Cedric Hanna, who tends the one at Matthew Town on Inagua in the Bahamas. ▲ Architecture is the way people structure their lives. Throughout the Bahamas and the Caribbean, the size and shape of African *bohios* is repeated in the chattel houses and other small homes. British and French architecture of the eighteenth and nineteenth centuries is reflected in the scaled-down adaptations of the Great Houses and important buildings. ► Stately flamingos flock to the salt flats on Inagua and Long Cay in the Bahamas, north of the Caribbean Sea, as well as to those of Bonaire, in the south, off the coast of Venezuela. ► ►

Finding a beach-fringed shore where your footprints can be the first may seem difficult, but it is not impossible on some of the Bahamas Family Islands and on many other islands throughout the Caribbean where coves are most easily found by boat. ◄ Boats for leisure time now claim shores long known to Arawaks and Caribs, followed by an assortment of explorers, pirates, settlers, and—most recently—tourists. ▲

Unique throughout the
Caribbean for its easy access and time-honored appeal
for those who climb its slippery rocks, Dunn's River Falls,
on Jamaica, is just west of the vacationer's town of Ocho
Rios, at a midpoint on the north coast. ▲ While some
Jamaicans make their living as guides for the climb up
the falls, others who live near the top of the waterfall use
the rocks and pools as their path to work in Ocho Rios. ▶

In the southern Bahamas, the young people of Inagua go to school in Matthew Town, where both history and prosperity are built on harvesting salt. ◄ Scraping the salt from flats, where the sun baked it from seawater, was backbreaking work for nineteenth-century workers. Today, Morton Bahamas Ltd. uses modern methods to create salt mountains from the business it bought from the Erikson family in 1954. ▲ Port Antonio, near the east end of Jamaica, has been the hideaway for Errol Flynn and countless other luminaries, but its natural attributes are its continuing appeal. ► ►

At the end of a dirt road, Jamaica's Reich Falls at Driver's River, east of Port Antonio, reward adventuresome travelers. ▲

Known as *balisier* in the French islands, *heliconia* hides its simple flower inside dramatic bracts. ▲ The decrepit remains of an outmoded lifestyle, Colonial buildings stand in Jamaica's Port Antonio and in other towns built by British settlers in the eighteenth and nineteenth centuries. They hold their secrets secure behind heavy wood doors, within brick and stucco walls that are several inches thick. ► ►

The British brought their custom of high tea, as well as Georgian architectural styles, to their colonies in the Caribbean. On independent Jamaica, where tourism is an important industry and a major employer, elegant resorts allow guests to sample a lifestyle seldom found in most people's daily lives. ▲

Haitians who walk their produce to and from the market are known as marchands; *they wear the "hat" of their trade.* ▲
Fishing is the traditional livelihood for those who are not merchants. ▶ ▶

Adapting a method used to bring fruit to market, rafters now take visitors along Jamaica's Rio Grande. ▲

In the 1940s, movie star Errol Flynn encouraged rafters to transport guests on their regular market journeys. ▲

Just as homes are decorated in the resident's taste, so handmade fishing boats in Jacmel, Haiti, show their owner's style. ▲

Traditional island boats were carved from the fat, straight trunk of the gommier tree, or sweated and then molded, plank by plank, to a handbuilt hull. The homesewn sails hang from tree-trunk masts, like laundry on the line, to billow with the trade winds and move the sailor through the seas. Leaving by the first light of dawn, the fishermen are back home by midday to sell their catch from the shore. ▲

The steady sun sets a languorous pace throughout the West Indies, especially in Haiti, which became the first Black Republic when it gained its independence from France in 1804. Battered by the vagaries of world economics, along with the country's own political leaders, Haitians manage to eke out a living from their land. Cap-Haitien, on the north, was separate from the rest of the country at the time when Henry Christophe built his astounding Citadelle, on the backbreaking work of thousands of his people. ▲

Haiti's future depends on its young people, who struggle against overwhelming odds to build a viable life. ▲
The people of the Caribbean have always mixed new customs with traditional patterns to create a unique lifestyle. ▶ ▶

Haitian crafts, including woven baskets, are essential for daily life as well as items for possible sale. ▲

The mortar which could hold the country of Haiti together is the confidence and ingenuity of its young people, if goals are made possible and met. Smiles are the universal language. ▲ Coffee brought propserity to Jacmel in the nineteenth century, when Frenchmen exported the high-quality beans that were in great demand for Europe's most elegant places. Storage houses built at that time—with arcaded doors to allow carriages to pass through and the wrought-iron balconies that were then popular—are used today, though the coffee industry has fallen on hard times. ► ►

In Old San Juan, Puerto Rico, open windows provide a balcony from which to watch the world pass by. ▲ When two or three gather together, in the islands, they are probably playing dominoes, as these men are in northern Haiti's Cap-Haitien. ▶ In 1797, advancing British abandoned their seige of Old San Juan when they saw Spanish reinforcements on the casement walls. In actual fact, the "forces" were torch-bearing women, chanting as they followed their Bishop in prayers. Old San Juan's statue on Plazuela de la Rogativa commemorates the event that saved the city. ▶ ▶

Spanish colonial architecture, with its thick walls and sturdy arches, has been restored throughout Old San Juan, Puerto Rico, an area now a living museum of the island's seventeenth- and eighteenth-century heritage. ◄ Festivities in Puerto Rico hark back to Spanish customs, with elements gathered from what has been learned of the early Taino culture. ▲

Old San Juan, Puerto Rico, built in the seventeenth and eighteenth centuries on a narrow peninsula, thrives in the twentieth century with buildings restored to hold cafes, galleries, small museums, and boutiques. Popular for shopping during daytime hours, the streets take on another personality in the evenings when there are street fairs and music. ▲

Puerto Ricans make the most of their festivals and competitions. ▲

San Felipe del Morro has been a landmark of San Juan, Puerto Rico, since Spaniards began the six-level fortress in 1540. ▲

The present structure of San Felipe del Morro dates from 1783, after extensive rebuilding and additions, most of which survived attack by Admiral Sampson's forces in the Spanish-American War. ▲ With walls rising 140 feet from the sea, El Morro fortress kept Old San Juan safe from the planned invasion by British forces led by Sir Francis Drake in 1595. Underground passageways, a compact historical museum, and a large center court all allow for a walk through history that can be as fascinating for adults as for children. ▶ ▶

Revered as a favorite sailing area, with landfalls including a spate of quiet islands and a few communities, the British Virgin Islands were known to European explorers and privateers from the 1600s through the 1800s. These days, it is visitors in search of natural surroundings who dive to historic shipwrecks and snorkel with colorful fish. Tortola's Brewers Bay is one of many quiet coves where yachtsmen anchor and intrepid land travelers enjoy the sun and the sea. ▲

Red roofs cap seventeenth- and eighteenth-century Danish dwellings on hillsides of Charlotte Amalie, St. Thomas. ▲
Undeveloped British and U.S. Virgin Islands recall sights Columbus might have seen when his ships sailed these seas. ▶ ▶

Burgeoning Charlotte Amalie, capital of the U.S. Virgin Islands, dots land and sea with homes. ▲

Brown pelicans provide entertainment, revving up their oddly-weighted bodies into flight and plunging from great heights to scoop fish-meals from the sea. ▲ Mill towers, talismen of sugar plantations of the eighteenth and nineteenth centuries, keep history alive on Caribbean hills. They are testimony to days when wind moved their sails and oxen worked the grinders at their base, as was the case at plantations on St. John, U.S. Virgin Islands, where this mill is preserved in the twenty-ninth U.S. National Park. ► ►

Throughout the British Virgin Islands are hundreds of remote, quiet coves best known to sailors on private or chartered yachts. Small boats give access to sugar-soft shores, where exploring is punctuated with snorkeling and swimming. Boulders in the sun-parched southern sector of Virgin Gorda hide sea pools where they meet the shore, at The Baths. ▲

The rock pools at The Baths on Virgin Gorda are best when nature is one's only companion. ▲

Although this Tortolan villa provides the shelter, the view of the British Virgin Islands is the raison d'etre. ▲

Acknowledged widely as the sailors' playpen, the many British Virgin Islands provide an ideal area for both novice and accomplished sailors. The trade winds are steady, landfall is never out of sight, and beach-fringed coves are within a few minutes' brisk sail when it is time to anchor. Sunsets gild these seas in shades that change each twilight; the sunrise, as a counterpoint, strips away the star-studded blackness to reveal another sparkling day in paradise. ▲

Following a tradition best known to the eighteenth-century pirates and privateers, twentieth-century cruising yachts provide comforts that were undreamed of by those earlier sailors. ▲ Best enjoyed at festivals—at Charlotte Amalie, St. Thomas, as well as on other islands—effervescence is natural to the West Indians, who have music in their souls and color in both their language and their clothing. ▶ With a dignity that masks their original purpose in earlier centuries as hideaways for pirate booty, the Danish-built warehouses of Charlotte Amalie, St. Thomas, are filled with luxury items from the world's marketplaces. ▶ ▶

In the Virgin Islands, when the seas are calm and the sun is setting, sailors have few cares. ◄ At Cane Garden Bay on Tortola, as elsewhere on the untrammeled islands of the Caribbean, the simple things in life yield the greatest pleasures. ▲ A flourishing port in Danish days, when its status as a free port made it a favorite for pirate treasure, Charlotte Amalie is a hive of shopping activity when cruise-ship vacationers and other travelers come to St. Thomas. ► ►

Although modern comforts ease the daily routine, it is still the natural marvels that become addictive throughout the Caribbean islands. The island magic comes from a sunrise, a sunset, the whisper of the trade winds as they pass palm fronds and other flora, the brilliance of a blossom in its sea of green foliage, and the anticipation of tales that could be told—if only the seas, the shores, and the skies could talk. ▲

Since the days of European explorers, barques and brigantines have shared sand-bordered coves with smaller craft. ▲
Boats as varied as their owners become a community as sun sets over Marigot, the main town on French St. Martin. ▶ ▶

Tranquility surrounds in a transparent sea off deserted Sandy Cay in the British Virgin Islands. ▲

A soft sunset over Cane Garden Bay, on Tortola in the British Virgin Islands, is wrapped in a thoughtful silence, broken only by the gentle slurp of waves against the shore and an occasional bird that calls before it settles for the night. And then the night chorus begins—tree frogs chirping their cricket-like song; the occasional skittering of a night creature; and the hoped-for rain shower, cooling and soothing the landscape before another day's relentless sunshine. ▲

Yachts at anchor in the tiny harbor at Terre de Haut, off Guadeloupe, hardly hint at nineteenth-century navel battles between the British and French that made the building of Fort Napoleon necessary. The sleepy town is best known to fishermen, some of whom have turned to innkeeping as their profession for the future. But the islands of Les Saintes remain— for now, at least—outside the mainstream of tourism. ▲

Reading the Caribbean seas is as crucial for yachtsmen today as it has been through the ages. ▲

In spite of a spate of development, Magen's Bay on St. Thomas remains one of the Caribbean's most beautiful strands. ▲

Once remote but now flecked with a resort, Dawn Beach, on the eastern shore of Dutch Sint Maarten, is a blanket of sand as soft as talcum powder. ▲ As is the case throughout most of the Caribbean countries, people on the two-nation island of Sint Maarten/St. Martin are a multiracial mix who yield international aspects. Love of the sea—and respect for its power and wealth—is born into every Caribbean person; an innate *joie de vivre* is a common trait. ► ►

Cafes, boutiques, and other gathering spots dot the border of Marigot's marina, creating a lively French seaside atmosphere unique to St. Martin. The area around the yacht harbor is as lively at nightfall, when the bistros and discos are alive, as it is in the early morning when hot coffee and croissants are a ritual for many who set out on their yachts at dawn. ▲

Within sight, but so different, tiny French St. Barthelemy is chic and style-setting. ▲
Dramatically different Dominica earns a sensational rainbow as the award for remaining natural. ▶ ▶

In its verdant hinterland, Dominica's waterfalls surprise intrepid travelers who hike to find them. ▲

A landmark for sailors since the time of Columbus, and perhaps before that, the Pitons of southern St. Lucia are visible for miles. Though the shoreline between them is now broken with an exclusive resort, the terrain stretching almost twenty-five hundred feet high is known only to experienced climbers who explore with knowledgeable St. Lucian guides. ▲ A beach near the one-time fishing village of Soufriere, at the base of the Pitons and not far from St. Lucia's sulphur springs, is a favorite landfall for sailors. ► ►

Religion is a vital force for most Caribbean people, especially those on mostly Catholic St. Lucia where the church is woven into the fabric of daily life. Religious teachings are integrated into schools, festivals, and rituals such as the first communion, an important ceremony for the entire family. Each village has its saint's day, with appropriate celebrations, and most islands have a long roster of important and colorful festivals that take their cue from an early religious event. ▲

Rocky coasts make portions of some Caribbean coastlines more dramatic than hospitable. ▲

A landmark for sailors, the dramatic peak of St. Lucia's Gros Piton rises above the fishing village of Soufriere. ▲

P igeon Island, which be-
came Pigeon Point when it was linked to St. Lucia by a
manmade causeway, is now Pigeon Point National Park.
With fortifications dating from the late 1700s—when the
British fought the French because of their support for
the American colonies—and a legend-filled history since
then, the area is popular for recreational activities such
as picnics, swimming, snorkeling, and scuba diving. ▲

The knowledge of fishing techniques is passed from one generation to the next; pride in his craft is part of an island fisherman's stock in trade. ▲ The Saturday morning market in Castries, the capital of St. Lucia, is as much a social occasion as it is a time to trade wares and produce. For most visitors, markets provide an opportunity to walk into the life of the country. ► The mountainous spine of St. Lucia is covered with verdant forests, which are maintained by the Forestry Department—and sometimes preserved, with hiking trails and nature walks, through the combined efforts of both Forestry and the National Trust. ► ►

Sam Lord's Castle, on the island of Barbados, is the centerpiece of a southeast coast resort and testimony to the entrepreneurial skills of a scoundrel. Lanterns, hung along his shoreline, lured ships heading for Bridgetown to his reef-fringed coast. Ship-wrecks yielded his wealth. ◄ Sam Lord's home, built in 1820 by English craftsmen, is furnished in Barbadian-Georgian style. High ceilings, louvered windows, and huge doorways permit trade-wind air-conditioning. ▲ Seas unchecked from the coast of Africa crash on the east coast of Barbados, which is surrounded by the Atlantic Ocean, although it shares the Caribbean lifestyle. ► ►

The natural colors of the tropical flowers and fruits add drama to the region's backdrop of sea blues and forest greens. ▲ Only a few avenues of royal palms still stand, although they once marked the entrance to the most prosperous plantations' Great Houses. On Barbados, the Codrington estate has become a respected boy's college, while other plantation houses are now museums, restaurants, and—in some cases—private homes. Sugar, the prized crop, still covers the midlands, although visitors are the "crop" that is cultivated along the west and south coasts of Barbados. ► The Caribbean seascape glistens in hundreds of shades from crystal clear to deepest sapphire, defined by the sun and the clouds as they play against coral, sand, and other parts of the underwater community far below. ► ►

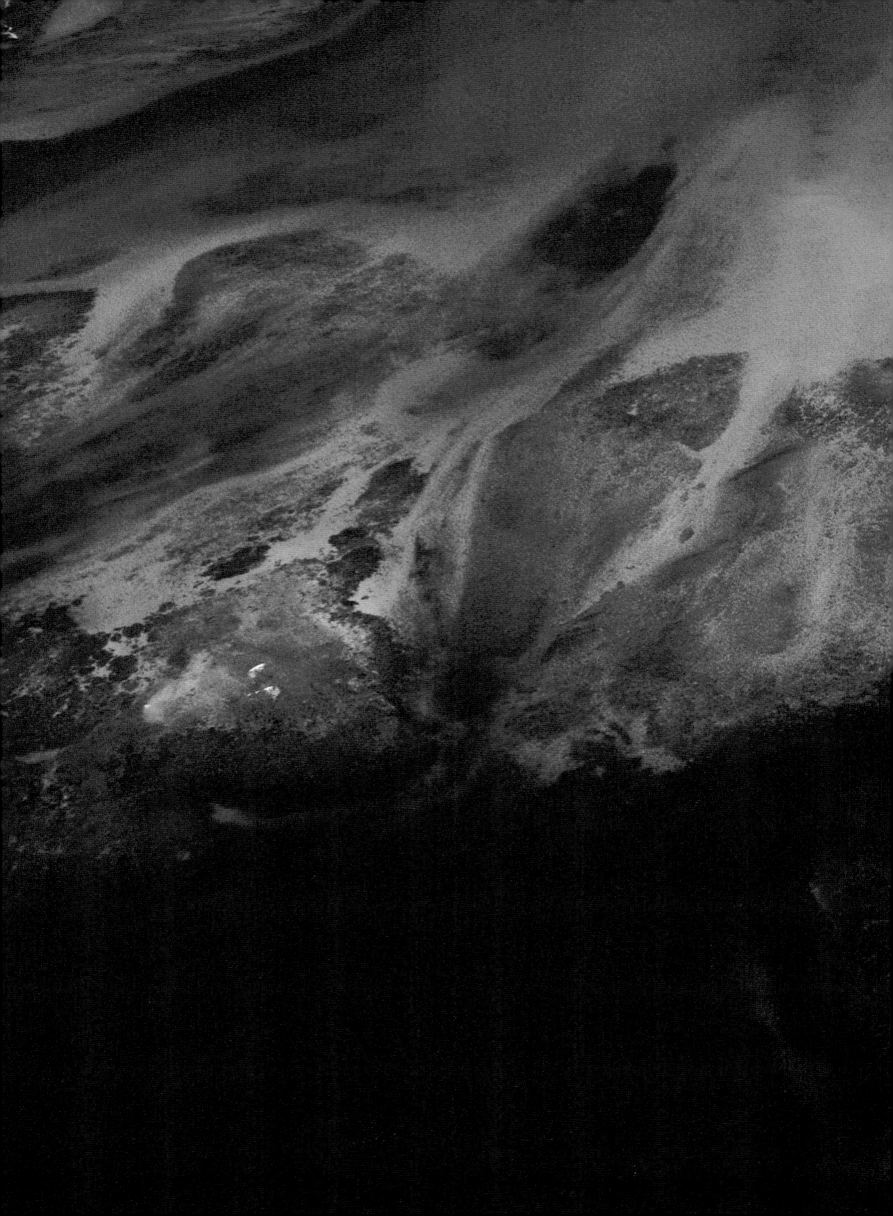

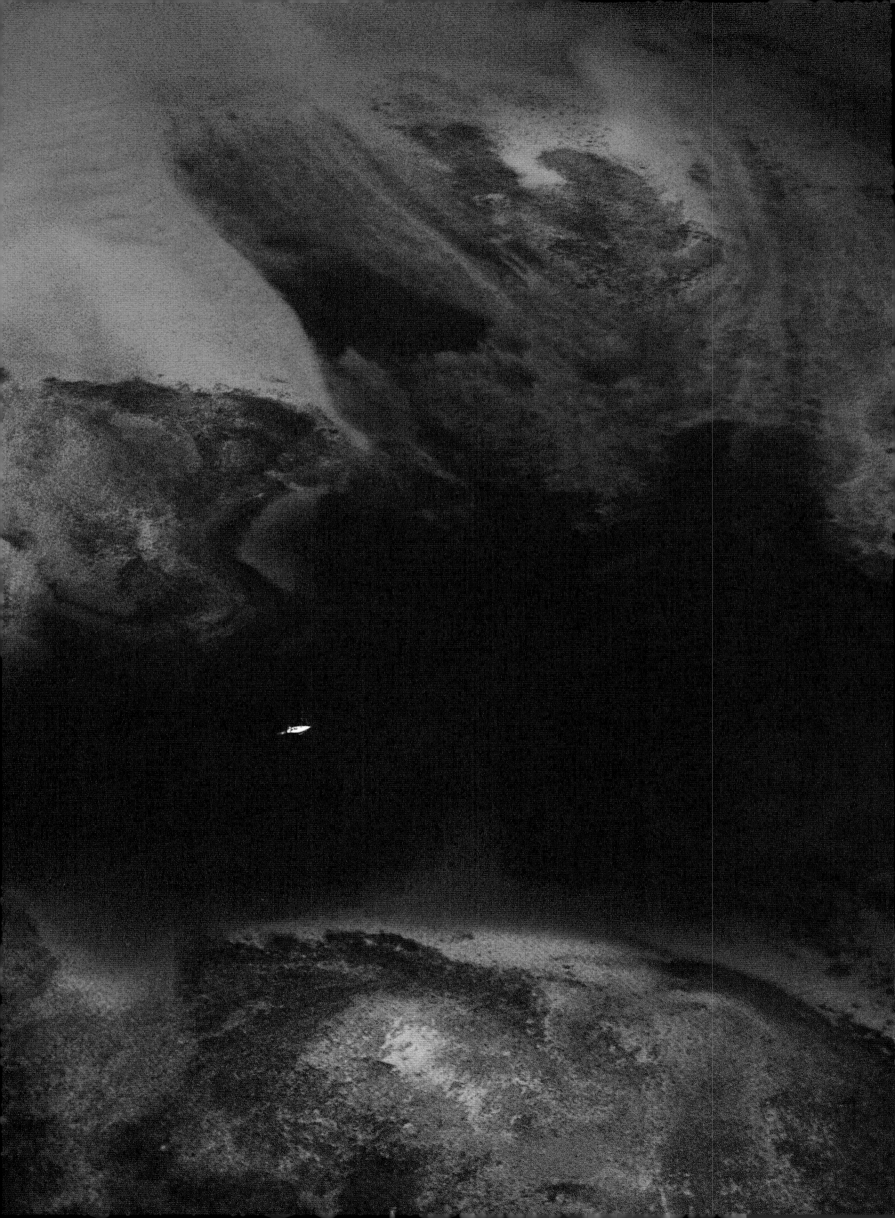

Dances, tracing their lineage to African tribes and mimicking movements from European courts, are woven into the cultural tradition of Caribbean people. On Carriacou, one of the Grenadine islands, the pulsating, agitated Big Drum dance is performed at festive occasions. ◄ Although St. George's market is open throughout the week, Saturday is the liveliest day, when Grenadians walk or take the occasional bus from far in the country to sell their produce and other products and buy what they need for the week ahead. Market day is a social event for local folk—and for some visitors who are welcome to mingle, look, and learn. ▲

Social occasions include all ages—and fill the days for many in country villages such as Sauters, on Grenada. ▲ Although the search for gold lured most explorers, spices brought riches to those who found the island of Grenada—and returned with nutmeg, cinnamon, mace, ginger, and cocoa for the tables of eighteenth-century Europe. Grenada grows one-third of the world's entire supply of nutmeg. When mace, the lace cover of the nutmeg seed, can be removed in one piece, it commands the highest price. ▶

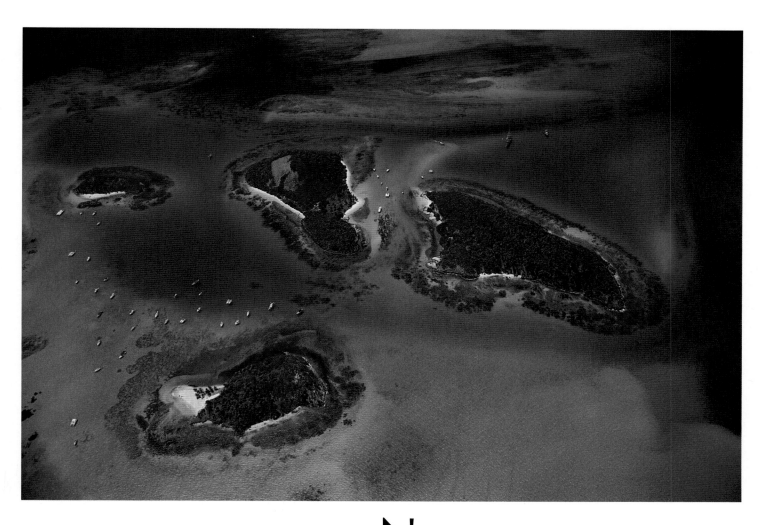

Nature gave the islands their greatest assets—flashes of brilliant color, from the Hibiscus and other flowers to the islands themselves. ◄ The Tobago Cays, members of St. Vincent's Grenadine islands, are slowly changing; the living coral that created them grows and modifies—and ever-increasing numbers of yachts anchor off their shores. ▲ The architecture of St. George's, the capital of Grenada, suggests the Georgian style that was popular in England at the time the town was settled. The waterfront and side streets are fringed with sun-baked eighteenth-century buildings that are now used for twentieth-century commerce. ► ►

Brilliant rouge-red scarlet ibis flock to Trinidad's Caroni Bird Sanctuary late each afternoon. ▲

Nesting in mangrove trees that have claimed the swampy area as their own, some three thousand scarlet ibis decorate the branches, providing colorful counterpoint to their green habitat. ▲ With Trinidad's northern peninsula stretching toward the coast of Venezuela, to which the island was once attached, Port of Spain, the capital, faces the sunset over the Gulf of Paria. The formerly British country braids numerous nationalities into its cosmopolitan culture. ▶ ▶

Cricket is in the soul of most West Indians with a British heritage, as it is with these Trinidadians. ▲

Symphonies are played by Trinidadians on pans, cut from steel oil barrels and tuned into tone bumps over fire. The musical instrument, created in the 1940s when U.S. servicemen worked with local groups, is now popular throughout the Caribbean, though Trinidad leads with classical music and sophisticated performances. ▲ The source of sustenance since time began, the sea is in the life of West Indians who look to it for food, a livelihood, and an avenue for travel. Only recently has it become a leisure playground. ▶ ▶

Trinidad sets the region's pace for fete, whether it be the annual pre-Lenten carnival or any one of the many other times when local folk prance and leap in the streets with a lively abandon that shakes away all problems and prejudices. ▲ Taking its cue from earlier times when costumes and acting were the only way for one-time slaves to communicate with each other, the elaborate dress for festive times is months in the making and always speaks its own language. ▶

Although photography is generally regarded as a solitary activity, there are always unseen hands along the way whose help and guidance bring a project like the CARIBBEAN to fruition. In my case, the aid came from many quarters, but especially from the magazine editors who were kind enough to send me to the region. I'd like to thank Bill Black and Adrian Taylor, then the picture editor and art director of *Travel & Leisure,* who gave me my first Caribbean assignment after I came back from a vacation in Haiti filled with enthusiasm for the area. In his current position as picture editor of *Travel/Holiday,* Bill also gave me my most recent Caribbean assignment, Dominica, for which I am most grateful.

Similar thanks are due to art director Albert Chiang and editor Joan Tapper, of *Islands* magazine, as well as Joan's predecessors, Nancy Zimmerman and Connie Bourassa-Shaw, for sending me south whenever possible. Hazel Hammond, Bob Ciano, Pamela Fiori, and Ila Stanger of *Travel & Leisure* and Veronica Stoddart of *Caribbean Travel & Life* have all contributed to this project, both in the form of assignments and display of this book in the pages of their fine publications. A project from Jon Fisher and John Nuhn of *International Wildlife* helped me to photograph the beautiful flamingos of Great Inagua.

I owe Gary Walther, now the editor of *Departures* magazine, a great deal of thanks for first putting the idea of a book about the Caribbean in my head, and then putting me in touch with the right people to publish it.

Ben Chapnick and the staff of Black Star have been stalwart supporters of this and many other projects since my early days as a newspaper photographer, as have John Jonny and Dick Bryant of Minolta Camera Company. For sharing their enthusiasm and knowledge of the islands they represent, and providing me with logistical support, I'd like to thank Marilyn Marx, Joan Bloom, Alison Ross, and Marcella Martinez.

And to the people of the Caribbean who helped me to explore their islands, I owe a special debt, especially Jimmy Nixon, Junia Brown, Henry Shackleford, Georgina Masson, and Alan Peltier.

BOB KRIST

The fabric of my life has been made by many people, dozens of whom are in or involved with the Caribbean. To all, I give a special "thank you," for showing me how to mix all the colors in a rainbow world so that each retains its special quality. I have grown up with the region, and continue to learn from the Caribbean family, as well as from my own family and friends, to whom I give heartfelt thanks for patience, enthusiasm, listening, calming, caring, and encouraging—as well as for the laughter and joy of shared experiences.

MARGARET ZELLERS